A Vision

by the Mother

Acknowledgement

All texts are the copyright of the Sri Aurobindo Ashram Trust, Pondicherry Mother India,
December 2010, January 2011, May 2011, June 2011, July 2011, October 2011,
November - December 2011

First edition 2021

ISBN 978-93-95460-19-4 (Paperpack)
ISBN 978-93-95460-18-7 (ebook)

BISAC Code:
PHI000000, PHILOSOPHY / General
PHI035000, PHILOSOPHY / Essays
PHI013000, PHILOSOPHY / Metaphysics
LCO022040, LITERARY COLLECTIONS / Subjects & Themes / Religious & Inspirational
JNF040000, JUVENILE NONFICTION / Philosophy

Thema Subject Category:
Q, Philosophy and Religion
QDTJ, Philosophy: metaphysics and ontology
QRVK, Spirituality and religious experience

Cataloging-in-Publication Data for this title is available from the Library of Congress.

Published by:
PRISMA, an imprint of Digital Media Initiatives
PRISMA, Aurelec / Prayogshala,
Auroville 605101, Tamil Nadu, India
www.prisma.haus

CONTENTS

Sketch for Mother's Painting "A Vision"

INTRODUCTIONS

On 28th May 1958, the Mother recounted a vision she once had of a wonderful Being of Love and Consciousness, emanated from the Supreme Origin and projected directly into the Inconscient so that the creation would gradually awaken to the Supramental Consciousness. The Mother's account of this vision was brought out a first time in November 1906 in the *Revue Cosmique*, a monthly review published in Paris. Six other visions followed in 1906 and 1907.

Although these accounts are unsigned, the fact that they begin with the same words, are written in the same style and develop on the same lines of experience, makes it almost certain that they are by the Mother.

In recounting her visions the Mother used a few terms taken from the "cosmic philosophy" expounded in the Revue. They have been rendered only approximately in translation so as to preserve the literary quality of the text. These terms are identified in the text by footnotes.

ONE OF
THE SEVEN VISIONS

Now I see a marvellous being...

I SLEPT and now I am awake.

I slept upon the western waters, and now I enter the ocean in order to explore its depths. Its surface is green as beryl, tinted silver by the moonlight. Beneath, the water is sapphire-blue and soon becomes faintly luminous.

I lay down upon undulations that shimmered like the ripples in moiré, and now I descend, rocked from one undulation to the next by a gentle regular motion, borne straight towards the west. As I glide downwards, the water grows more luminous and is streaked with wide silvery currents.

Thus I go on descending for a long time, rocked from undulation to undulation, down and ever further down.

Suddenly, looking upward, I notice a gleam of pink; I draw nearer and see a coral-like shrub, as large as a tree, clinging to a blue rock. Water creatures come and go in countless variety. Now I stand on the fine bright sand. I look around me in wonder. There are mountains and valleys, fantastic forests, strange flowers which could almost be animals, fish one could take for flowers - there is no separation, no interval between stationary and moving beings. Everywhere are colours, soft or vivid and iridescent, yet always refined and in harmony with one another. I walk on golden sand and gaze at all this beauty, which is bathed in a faint pale-blue radiance dotted with tiny circling spheres, red or green or golden.

How marvelous are the depths of the sea! Everywhere one feels the presence of the One in whom all harmonies dwell!

I continue westwards, with no fatigue or lessening of speed. Scene follows scene in incredible variety; there, on a rock of lapis-lazuli, are fine and delicate sea-weeds, like long blond or violet hair; here are great rose-coloured walls, all spangled with silver; there are flowers which seem carved from enormous diamonds; and here are goblets as fine as if they had been wrought by the most skilful of craftsmen, containing what look like drops of emerald throbbing with alternate pulsations of shadow and light.

Now I have entered on a path of silver sand between two walls of rock as blue as sapphire; the water becomes more clear and luminous.

Suddenly, at a turn in the path, I find myself before a cave which appears to be made of wrought crystal, all sparkling with rainbow light.

Between two iridescent columns stands a tall being; his face is that of a very young man, and is framed with short *fair curls; his eyes are as green as the sea. He wears a light-blue tunic, and on his shoulders are great snow-white fins in place of wings. On seeing me, he stands back against a column to let me pass. Hardly have I crossed the threshold when an exquisite melody strikes my ears. Here the water is all iridescent, the ground is strewn with nacreous pearls; the entrance and the vault, from which graceful stalactites are hanging, are like opal, and delectable perfumes fill the air. Galleries, nooks and recesses open on every side, but straight in front of me I see a great light, and towards that I direct my steps. This light is made of wide rays of gold, silver, sapphire and emerald and ruby, all issuing from a point too distant for me to distinguish what it is, and streaming out in all directions. I feel myself being drawn towards their centre by a powerful attraction.*

Now I can see the source of these rays and I behold an oval of white light, haloed by a splendid rainbow. The oval is lying horizontally, and I sense[1] that the one whom the light hides from my view is deep in sleep. I stand long at the outer edge

---

1. *Sentienter:* to be aware with all the senses (physical and subtle) together.

of the rainbow, peering through the light to see the one who lies sleeping in such splendour. Unable to distinguish anything in this way, I enter first the rainbow, and then the shining white oval. Now I see a marvellous being, lying on what seems to be a mass of white down; his lithe, incomparably beautiful body is clothed in a long white robe. Of his head, which rests on his folded arm, I can see only his long locks, the colour of ripe grain, flowing down over his shoulders. A powerful and sweet emotion floods through me at this magnificent sight, and also a profound reverence.

Has the sleeper sensed[2] my presence? Now he awakes, and rises in all his grace and beauty. He turns towards me and his eyes meet mine, eyes that are mauve and shining, full of infinite sweetness and tenderness. Without a word, he bids me a loving[3] welcome, to which my whole being joyously responds; then, taking me by the hand, he leads me to the couch he has just left. I lie down upon this downy whiteness and the harmonious visage leans over me. A sweet flow of force suffuses me entirely, vitalising, revivifying each cell.

---

2. ditto.
3. Pathitique: full of divinised love.

Then, surrounded by the splendid rainbow hues, wrapped in soothing melodies and exquisite perfumes, beneath that powerful and tender gaze, I fell asleep in a beatific repose. And in my sleep I learned many beautiful and useful things.

Of all the marvelous things that I understood without the sound of words, I shall mention only one.

Wherever there is beauty, wherever there is radiance, wherever there is progress towards perfection, be it in the Heavens of the heights or in the Heavens of the depths, there, surely, beings will be found in the form and likeness of man - man, the supreme agent of terrestrial evolution.

SECOND OF THE SEVEN VISIONS

I see a young boy of about fourteen years...

I SLEPT and now I am awake. I am travelling swiftly towards the east, borne along by a small violet cloud which completely envelops me and prevents me from seeing anything on the way.

After a while I feel myself being set gently upon the ground, and the cloud withdraws; I am standing beside a high white wall. As I look at it, I see shadows creeping stealthily along the wall - men passing one behind the other at a distance, as if they did not wish to be observed. They are dressed in long violet tunics, with round hoods pulled down over their heads, concealing their faces almost completely. One after the other they disappear through a little door in the wall. Invisible to all, I follow them to see where they are going with such caution.

After passing through a small bare white room I find myself in a courtyard surrounded by arches and planted with orange-trees bearing their fine golden fruits. At the centre of the courtyard there is a fountain, with a basin of opulent blue, green and white mosaic, spouting a thin stream of water. The murmur of the fountain is the only sound that breaks the silence, for the courtyard is deserted; I cross it and pass through two more rooms, which also are empty. Finally I reach a staircase, and I climb up it onto a square terrace.

In a corner I see, reclining on cushions, a man half-veiled by an aura of splendid crimson, full of tiny moving golden sparkles. The man rises. He is a fine looking old man; both his hair, visible beneath a violet cap, and his beard are as white as snow; his bearing is noble and dignified. He is dressed in an ample violet robe girdled with a crimson belt; in his hand he holds a pair of golden scissors. He seems to be waiting for someone.

And now, even as I observe the old man, the men whom I saw creeping along the wall enter one by one. In silence they range themselves in a circle around the edge of the terrace, and after them come others dressed in white, who go and stand in front of the first-comers.

All are motionless, all are silent. The one who appears to be their leader stands, very solemn, facing the head of the staircase. Gradually a soft glow pervades the air, shedding its light upon the still figures; as I turn round to identify the source of this light, I see a young boy of about fourteen years climbing the stairs that lead to the terrace; he is surrounded by a beautiful white radiance in which iridescent gleams can be seen. His flaxen hair falls in shapely curls upon his shoulders; his complexion is fair and delicate; his long eyelashes rest upon rose-tinted cheeks, for his eyes are downcast. He is dressed in a pale azure robe, girdled with a white silken cord, and wears sandals on his feet. Drawing forward slowly, he comes to a standstill one step away from the old man, and bows his head in silence. Then the old man speaks in a deep, gentle voice, but he speaks in a language unknown to me and I do not understand ...

I have slept, and now I understand the meaning of the old man's words. He tells the child, "Thus you are about to fulfil the task entrusted to you, which you have accepted of your own free will; you will accomplish it in accordance with the instructions I have given you, without fear or weakness, for you know that we are one and that neither our love[1] and that neither or love nor our protection will ever fail you. You know the magnitude of the work you are about to perform, as well as all the pitfalls and dangers you will no doubt meet on your way; but be of good heart, for though the struggle be arduous, the victory is sure. You shall proceed towards the west, my child. May our highest blessing be with you."

------

1. *Pathetisme*: divinised love.

Saying these words, he bends forward and impresses a deep kiss upon the white brow of the adolescent; then with the golden scissors he snips off one of the beautiful flaxen locks and slips it under his robe.

Then, without word or gesture, the child slowly and solemnly turns, and re-descends the stairs that lead to the terrace. I follow him, and see him leave the house and walk swiftly along the wall, his head high, looking straight before him.

Suddenly I find myself enveloped once more in the cloud, which bears me away, hiding everything from my sight. Once only does it open again, allowing me to look with wonder on a great river, its waters flowing silver beneath the moonlight, its banks overgrown with a splendid and luxuriant vegetation. Everything here is on a gigantic scale: the river that is broad as a lake, the trees with their crests that seem to touch the sky and behind, the mountains stretching out of sight, their summits covered with perpetual snow.

In the midst of this immensity I see a tiny oval of moving white light; it is the child walking firmly and surely upon his way, his head high, without fear or weakness.

This scene is full of grandeur; I contemplate it and muse, I muse and understand: what a man at the height of his strength would find hard to achieve if he were alone, a child can accomplish almost without difficulty if he is sustained by the power and love[2] of those who are one with him.

Surely indeed, hierarchic grouping by affinity is the path that leads to victory!

2. Ditto

THIRD OF
THE SEVEN VISIONS

Awake, O evolving supermen...

I SLEPT and now I am awake.

I awoke in the great austere cathedral of the most intellectual of European capitals. I awoke to the sound of majestic organ strains, strains rising and unfolding in the huge nave like a puissant call, a noble aspiration. Looking up, I see seated at the manual a young fair-haired woman in white raiment. As her fingers touch the keys, the harmonies soar one after another, inspired and full of love.[1]

Looking down, I see that gradually the cathedral is filling with an eager throng attracted by the ample strains which can be heard outside. At the same time I see the organ gallery filling slowly with an increasingly brilliant light; the light spreads throughout the edifice, dispelling the darkness. A great dazzling white light falls upon the altar, and when it has dispersed a little, the cross, the religious images, the objects of worship have disappeared, as if pulverized by an invisible hand.

All present are rooted to the spot, divided between surprise, curiosity and fear. Their amazement increases when they see a great violet veil forming and growing denser before

---

1. *Pathetique:* full of divinised love.

the choir and, appearing on the veil, letters of golden light tracing the following inscription for all to read:

The Self is your God.

You are the living Temple of the Divine Inhabitant.

Awake, O evolving supermen.[2]

Evolve, develop your latent faculties

so as to realise the indissoluble union

of God, the Unthinkable Absolute,

with eternal Substance

through Man, regenerated and glorious,

immortal upon earth, his rightful home.

The wonderment reaches a climax; in the silence that none dares to break, rises a deep ringing voice, saying, "Hearken to the teaching of the music." I turn my gaze towards the organ, but no longer see the young woman, who is now completely veiled by a brilliant light. At the far end, silhouetted against the multi-coloured rosette, I see a seraph thrice as tall as a man;

---

2. *Psycho-intellectuels:* men evolving into the divine supermen.

he stands in his sapphire tunic with two of his wings crossed above his fine young head, two outstretched behind his arms, and two lying upon the ground and covering his feet.

Once more the organ strains rise, at first sombre and tumultuous, imaging the present condition of man in his misery and suffering and doubt; then suddenly a crystalline note is heard, piercing the sorrowful phrase as a spark of light pierces the gloom; the clear and pure melody unfurls, grows louder, stronger; a struggle begins between it and the fierce, disorderly strains, which gradually fade and die away, overpowered and drowned by the calm chant which spreads and ripples like a tranquil sea.

Suddenly a rich warm voice intones a powerful hymn: "Appear, O light, sublime intelligence, redeemer of the world!"

The billows of music roll with a growing force and rapture, filling the edifice with wonderful notes, shaking the stained-glass windows with their joyful, resonant waves. Once more the voice is heard: "Arise, O regenerated man, sublime man, manifest the divine intelligence, celebrate the grand eternal nuptials, radiate love, pure love, universal love - love, the supreme harmony; arise in thy strength and knowledge, O all-powerful master of thy physical realm, realiser of equilibrium!

Honour, honour to thee, O man divine and human, man immortal and glorious!"

The last strains of the triumphal hymn loose forth their dazzling notes in a hush of rapt admiration. A deep calm broods over the congregation. The huge vault is draped in a luminous amethyst cloak and, spread beneath it, is a veil of living emerald: sapphire stars are scintillating and moving everywhere; near the organ, thirty-six winged beings have placed themselves beside the seraph, forming a sapphire circle around the brilliant white aura that veils the young inspired one.

Slowly and silently, the throng flows out in wonder; the sick are healed, the anxious and the uneasy are soothed and reassured, the weak are strengthened, the intelligent are enlightened. And as they depart, all carry away with them, indelibly impressed upon their memories, the magnificent inscription penned in letters of gold.

FOURTH OF
THE SEVEN VISIONS

In a distance the floating house appears...

I SLEPT and now I am awake.

I awoke in the middle of a populous city, in a great, cheerfully-lit hall where a feast is being held. Around a long, richly-laden table, a dozen people are sitting and talking merrily. At the centre I see an old man with a fine noble head enframed by a great beard and long silky white hair; his expression is at once very grave and very gentle, and even his gaiety has a touch of solemnity. Beside him sits a young, fair-haired woman dressed in flowing white veils. The ten others are men, disciples gathered around their master.

While the feast goes on joyfully, I feel and see gathering slowly above the town a heavy cloud charged with hostility.

The young woman too has sensed[1] the impending danger; she suddenly rises and speaks in an inspired voice: "A great calamity broods over us, a dreadful cataclysm is in the making. I sense it although I cannot say exactly what it is; we must at all costs leave the town immediately, together with all who trust us and are willing to follow us." None of those present doubts the grave words that have disturbed the

---

1. *Sentientier:* to be aware with all the senses (physical and subtle) together.

harmonious gathering; all rise unhesitatingly and prepare to leave the hall.

At that moment the scene fades from my sight and for a while I can discern nothing more. As soon as my consciousness returns, I find the little group again, but how the scene has changed!

The twelve have left the town, which is now only ruins and destruction. How violent the upheaval must have been! For nothing remains of this huge city but heaps of rubble, so consumed by fire and eroded by water that they seem even now to have lain there for centuries. Earthquake, eruption, flood, all three must have contributed to change the product of so much science and art so abruptly and totally into grey or red rock-like mounds and hillocks all blackened by smoke. Not a blade of grass remains to be seen, and in the midst of this vast wasteland runs a wild torrential flood sweeping away all kinds of wreckage in its rapid course. Above this agonising scene stretches a beautiful expanse of cloudless, limpid blue sky, which seems to mock this wretched earth.

Along the arid banks, beside the turbulent waters, are encamped thousands of people driven from the town by the fury of the elements. They are plunged in listless despair, sitting with idle arms and empty looks, or pacing jerkily back and forth; the shock has been too great for them and seems to have jolted them out of their senses.

By contrast, the little group has remained calm and courageous; the master is walking beside the torrent, his protective arm around the young woman, surrounded by his trusting disciples. They feel for the lot of this bewildered crowd and grieve at their inability to help them. The old man knows that they must leave the place with all possible speed, for the danger still threatens; fresh upheavals are bound to occur and perhaps all will be flooded. So he advances towards the crowd and explains in a loud clear voice how to use the driftwood littering the ground to build rafts which will enable them to flee the imminent disaster. Then, after a last sad farewell to the collectivity, the little group makes its way to a sort of floating house waiting for them moored to a rock. The twelve board this makeshift boat; one of them shoves off with a pole and they launch forth upon the torrent which bears them away at a tremendous speed amid the rocks and the flotsam of all kinds strewing its course.

They hasten on and on at a dizzy speed. The young woman in white raiment stands near to an opening in the broadside, gazing upon the scene outside and keeping watch. A young man says, "If we can only reach the sea, all will be well."

Another replies, "That will be difficult, for near to the sea there is a reef and we might be dashed to pieces on the rocks." Then the voice of the master rises deep and majestic, "You know full well that our dwelling can never sink: is it not the symbol of eternal truth?" Several men reply in unison, pointing to the young woman who is still standing, "Besides, so long as she is here in our midst, no harm can befall us." And she watches ever more intently.

Suddenly, after covering a great distance, the floating house comes in view of what must once have been a very large and beautiful city. Only huge pieces of wall, and the ruins of steeples and spires and palaces, are visible, eaten away by air and wind, water and fire, their weird white shapes pointing to the sky. The ground is hidden by running water, and at the centre of the town, which must once have been the site of a river or a vanished harbour, lie great sailing ships of which only bare hulks remain.

The scene is so impressive and brings to mind so vividly the idea of a great civilisation destroyed, that all gaze in *silence, in grave and sorrowful contemplation.*

At that moment all fades once more from my sight, and when I become conscious again, I find myself above the sea, a wild tumultuous sea swollen with huge billows ready to swallow up all that would be so rash as to draw near them. Amid these waves I see beings of disorder, ferocious and grimacing, who with their own power are increasing the power of the raging waters. Looking more closely, I realise that their frenzy is aimed at some crimson figures whom they wish to seize, but who oppose them by their very calm; yet soon, perhaps, their strength will be exhausted.

Then in the distance the floating house appears, profiled in violet against the foamy sea. It glides upon the waters on a straight, even course, as upon a perfectly smooth surface; and indeed, fore and aft of the boat, amid the waves that grow suddenly calm at its approach, a long silver path, luminous and smooth, unfolds. On either side of the path the waves rise sheer like walls, but a powerful force prevents them from bearing down upon the refuge of the little group. And now, one by one, the crimson figures emerge from the water in defiance of the violent efforts of their enemies, and take shelter in the floating house. As soon as all are safe, the huge waves fall back upon themselves, rolling, crushing, swallowing up the hostile beings who oppose them in vain.

Gradually all becomes peaceful again; the water, with scarcely a ripple upon its surface, turns sapphire blue; the sky is ablaze with sunlight, and the boat goes on its way haloed in white light.

Within, all rejoice. The little group has given a loving[2] welcome to those they have saved, and the master says in his deep gentle voice, "Thus it is that sooner or later, light shall triumph over darkness, order over disorder, love over hate, and harmony reign over a Universe at peace!"

---

2. *Pathetique:* full of divinised love.

FIFTH OF
THE SEVEN VISIONS

Queen of the isles of the deep waters...

I SLEPT and now I am awake.

I awoke in the remote past, beside a pool with waters of deep sapphire, as calm as a mirror.

To the east of the lake I see a magnificent grove of rare species of trees and shrubs, whose long outcurving branches play upon the surface of the still, limpid water, reflecting bright flowers of rich and variegated colours. In the shade of this charming natural retreat bloom splendid white lotuses.

The whole retreat is radiant with rainbow light, and the centre of this radiance is a young, fair-haired medium asleep in her graceful beauty, reclining upon the wide flat leaves, her head resting against one of the beautiful five-petalled flowers. Her ample white garment is girdled with a golden belt.

On her left, erect and proud, like a vigilant sentry, stands a white ibis perching on one of its coral legs. Above the sleeper hangs a protective mantle of dark amethyst. A calm and serene beatitude pervades the scene. The medium[1] seems to be resting in an enchanting dream.

A sweet fresh breeze rustles the leaves and gently ruffles the waters; with its caressing breath it seems to

---

1. *Psycho-intellectuels*: men evolving into the divine Supermen.

murmur, "Queen of the isles of the deep waters." - "Queen of the isles of the deep waters" echoes a melodious voice rising from the fathomless sapphire depths.

Then I fell asleep, and I awoke in the vast hall of a palace.

From the shape and ornamentation of the columns, the paintings that embellish the walls with such lavishness and yet restraint, I gather that I am in one of the superb palaces of ancient Egypt, at Memphis or Thebes.

The hall is filled with a picturesque crowd; the brightly-coloured loin-cloths, the feather head-dresses, the jewels, the hangings all form a rich and curious harmony. Every gaze is turned towards the north end of the hall, in the middle of which stands a throne raised upon twelve steps and crowned with a velvet canopy. At the foot of the steps lie two young lions like two strong and peaceful guardians. At the left of the throne a white ibis stands on its pink legs. The throne itself is wrapped in dazzling light, and at the centre of this light I see the young, fair-haired medium with a white lotus in her left hand.

Each of those present passes in turn, bows before the steps and swears an oath of allegiance.

For a second time I fell asleep, and when I awake I find myself before a temple in the strange and sumptuous Hindu style. Kneeling stone elephants support the pillars on either side of the square door. The door is open, and men in long white, blue, violet or scarlet robes, enter singly or in groups. I follow them, and after crossing several vestibules, I come to a small square hall with a dark amethyst vault supported by thirty-six mighty pillars. The men assemble in order of function and rank, and remain silent; they are waiting for someone. Suddenly the curtain that screens one end of the hall is lifted, revealing a veiled figure of brilliant light. The figure steps forward and takes its stand at the centre of the circles of the hierarchy. I recognise the young medium. The only ornament she wears is a white lotus flower in her loose blond hair; she is dressed in a long white tunic girdled with a golden sash.

Once again all fades from my sight. Upon waking, I find myself in the midst of a vast oak forest. In the distance, between the tall tree-trunks, one glimpses the green sea burning copper in the setting sun. I feel that I am on a Western Isle.

Through the coppice I see advancing a long line of virgins in white raiment; those leading the column hold musical instruments in their hands and wend their way forward chanting to the sound of the lyre and the timbrel. Then the maidens join hands and begin to dance; they pass *by, weaving a circle around the oak at the centre, which is taller and stouter than the others.*

Attended by four of her companions, now comes the young, fair-haired medium[2]. She holds a golden sickle in her hand and moves forward with a solemn and meditative step. At the foot of the ancient oak she stops and hands her sickle to a young boy who has come with her. He nimbly climbs the tree. With a single stroke he cuts the great ball of parasitic mistletoe, which falls into the tunic that the young girl has held out to catch it.

Then, resuming their melodious chant, the maidens return the way they came. I fall asleep for the fourth time, and upon waking I recognise the unique, wonderful setting of the Queen of the Adriatic at the finest hour of her royalty.

Venice, the strange and untamed - Venice, the city of art and of reckless passion - Venice, with crime oozing from her walls and drama exuding from her canals ... Here are the magnificent palaces in all the splendour of their flourishing youth; here are the graceful gondolas carrying gentle ladies and great lords in fine array.

---

2. *Passive:* Medium open to the higher subtle planes

But I am drawn by a powerful inner sensation[3] *towards the Ducal Palace; I know that there I shall find the one whom I have just seen down the centuries.*

I enter the great courtyard; and there indeed, near the Staircase of the Giants, half-hidden behind a column, I see the young fair-haired medium[4] *dressed in a white robe. She clings to the shoulder of a fine-looking old man who has his arms around her, as if to protect her. Their faces are sorrowful, their bearing solemn. Thus clasped together, they watch a gorgeous procession slowly mounting the steps that lead to the palace. And it is clear to me that their fate lies in the hands of these men, who are their mortal enemies.*

Then the old man bends forward and kisses the brow of the child, saying gravely, "Many aeons we have struggled and suffered for the sacred cause and the salvation of mankind, in many varied lands and changing circumstances.

"Once again we have attempted our sublime endeavour, and it cannot be in vain. The enemies of man may now be

---

3. *Sentientiation*: being aware with all the senses (physical and subtle) together.
4. *Passive*: Medium open to the higher subtle planes.

stronger than we, but our time will inevitably come. They work for division and falsehood; we belong to those who struggle and have always struggled for Truth and Harmony; these alone are immortal. The more arduous the battle, the fairer the victory. Effort matters little when the outcome is sure."

And the child replies in a gentle voice, "Indeed it is so, and I am certain that upon our next coming to earth we shall witness the Victory!".

SIXTH OF
THE SEVEN VISIONS

Indeed, four eagles appear...

I SLEPT and now I am awake.

I awoke on the threshold of a long, vaulted path; this path is formed of great transparent emerald-green undulations, flowing like ripples upon the still surface of water into which a stone has been cast. The luminous sapphire-blue vault is supported by two rows of small slender pillars of some substance like lapis-lazuli; between the pillars a pale emerald light can be seen, as if all this were at the bottom of a tranquil green sea.

I am drawn towards this path, stretching as far as the eye can see, and I enter upon it. The ripples bear me along in a swift rhythmical motion, and so I continue for a long time. The motion accelerates as I move onwards - I must have travelled a very great distance. The journey seems interminable, for I am longing to see what is at the end of this path. Suddenly I distinguish a luminous white point. By an effort of will I increase my speed, and as I draw near I see that this point is a white square; when I reach its base it is immense. Then, a little weary from the journey, I lie down and fall asleep. While I sleep, my intelligence awakens and I understand what I have just seen. I understand that this path, vaulted with blue and paved with emerald undulations, is the way of intellectual evolution open in life to men of goodwill, the long but radiant path that leads all who wish to the four-fold equilibrium.

Having understood this, I awake refreshed and strengthened, for I have rested in the purple overshadow. I sense that I am about to see what at first was hidden to me by the white square.

Indeed, four eagles appear; they are dark blue, sitting back to back in a square and facing the four cardinal points. They bear upon their heads a small tablet, above which rises a white cloud. Beyond the cloud shines a very bright light. After contemplating the light I turn my gaze back to the eagles and see that they have become white and faintly radiant. While looking at them I fall asleep, and again my intelligence awakens to the understanding of what I have just seen.

The eagles, who are at first in affinity with my mental vision - hence their blue colour - face the four cardinal points because they are turned towards life and light, light and power, power and utility, utility and light. In other words, they await the realisation of perfectioning in life so that life may become ready for the permanent individualisation of intelligence; and they await the perfection of individualised intelligence so that it may become fit for exercising power, the *power that is to manifest in and through utility, that is to be used for the perfection of earth and man. And this will allow mankind to lift the veil represented by the cloud and attain a higher intelligence, a light of dazzling brightness; by this light man will see with a balanced vision - a vision at once full of love,[1] spiritual, intellectual and vital - the eagles which symbolise the intermediaries between the evolving supermen[2] and the higher radiances.*

As soon as I have received this explanation my eyes open once more and I see, outlined against a dark-blue square, a sphere divided into two equal parts, one white and very luminous, the other a beautiful dark violet.

Having slept, I understand that I have passed from the vision of possibilities to the vision of the means of realisation. In mental equilibrium I contemplate earth, our heritage, our home by eternal right, balanced between light and power[3] between intellectual radiance and the protective overshadow. Earth, not as it is now, but charged with

---

1. *Pathetique:* full of divinised love.
2. *Psycho-intellectuels:* men evolving into the divine supermen.
3. *Auriser:* to change with spiritual light and power.

spiritual light and power by the evolving supermen[4] arranged in hierarchical order.

My calm is deep and still, my hope immense, my aspiration intense, and for the fourth time I awake. I see a square portal of deep amethyst, supported by two strong white pillars. In the middle of the doorway, on the ground, two violet eagles sit side by side, closely united. One faces east the other faces west.

Above their heads, at the centre of the portal, shines a splendid white sun all radiant with iridescent beams.

I gaze upon this wonderful scene with a profound delight. It feels as if one of the beautiful sunbeams has entered my head; all is illumined within me. This portal is the entrance opening upon victorious realisation, and this entrance is power in equilibrium, in duality, more rarefied and radiant.

In the middle of this entrance, not soaring in space but standing upon firm ground, the dual eagles in sovereign purple represent power in utility - terrestrial might. They are united by the indissoluble bond of affinity, and yet one faces in the direction of the setting sun, the other towards the rising

---

4. *Psycho-intellectuels:* men evolving into the divine supermen.

sun, like a symbol of repose and awakening, of passivity and activity, which must be rightly balanced for one to rise from one level to another, to ascend from light to ever purer and more radiant light.

Only by this equilibrium can the iridescent beams of the splendid white sun, centre of all forces, be fully utilised by the children of earth, who thirst for its magnificent illumination whose splendour is increasing and will go on increasing for ever!

SEVENTH AND FINAL VISIONS

I see a rider mounted on a splendid white horse...
Restitution...

I SLEPT and now I am awake.

I am awake and I see a rider mounted on a splendid white horse. The rider wears a breast-plate of glittering gold and flourishes a sword, whose naked blade shines with a sapphire gleam. With one tremendous bound, the horse leaps across a chasm of darkness.

As I marvel at this vision, I hear a word, a single word pregnant with hope and promise: "Restitution."

Then suddenly a breach appears in the gloomy chasm and a great path is formed, like a dazzling rainbow. A white dove with crimson feet is ascending this path, and as I watch it on its way I behold a wonderful scene beyond the darkness.

In faultless hierarchical order, clad in sparkling light and armed with double-edged swords, an immense host is deployed, ready for battle. They await a signal from the leader at their centre, who is all radiant with iridescent light. But at once my gaze is drawn to a young man whose height and majesty tower above all the others. An ample amethyst cloak, lined with dazzling white, falls from his shoulders.

All stand still in rapt silence, for he is about to speak. He speaks, and his voice rises solemn and sweet. He speaks, and I understand what he is saying: "The time draws near. Let all prepare themselves, the host of earth and the host of heaven. Let those who work and endure lose neither courage nor patience. Though invisible to all but a few, the work is proceeding swiftly. On one side a growing order and harmony is driving towards the denser spheres whatever confusion and disorder still prevail. On the other hand, upon earth, the seed which has been sown is ready to rise amid a field of men of ardent and enlightened goodwill. The valiant host of evolving supermen[1] is making ready so that when the time comes its efforts may be joined to ours. Soon a hymn of joy shall ring forth, the paean of triumph and glory."

Rejoicing in these words, I make my way back towards earth, bearing the glad tidings, and in my descent I am followed by the white dove with crimson feet.

After passing the dark chasm, I look back and I see ... Oh, what do I behold! ...

---

1. *Psycho-intellectuels:* men evolving into the divine Supermen.

The dark heavy cloud is supported by a huge cross, and both cloud and cross are borne by a being of colossal size. The entire burden of iniquity and disorder weighs upon him, who leans over mankind like a wonderful and living protection. His long hair falls on either side of his beautiful face, which is turned towards earth with a look of infinite tenderness and pain ...

Oh yes! all must work with ardour and energy to hasten the hour when the awesome effort of this sublime man will no longer be needed to hold the dark cloud in check and prevent it from crushing the wretched men of earth, unawakened and as yet unable to defend themselves!

Let all men of goodwill join together, let all efforts be united, let all living beings awaken to intelligence, let all in whom the light shines awaken to spirituality and love, the love that is harmony and order and supreme impersonality, so that soon may ring forth the hymn of joy, the paean of triumph and glory!

BIRTH OF THE GODS AND THE GODDESSES

Sweet Mother, how were the gods and goddesses born?

BUT it is precisely. . . it is part of the creation. What we call "Aditi" here, that is, the Creative Consciousness, well, the Creative Consciousness . . .

I am going to tell you about this in an absolutely childish way:

She formed at first four beings; when she received the mission to create she put out four emanations from her being; and these four emanations were made and given the charge to develop the universe. And then — I think I have already spoken to you about this once — it turned out badly, we could put it like that; and so when things went wrong, she made another creation of all the beings who became the gods; and parallel to the disorder created by the first four emanations, there was the development in order, that is, under the guidance of the Supreme, the creation in order of all the worlds descending further and further towards Matter. And it is to this line that the gods belong who were manifested later, a formation, a greater and greater materialisation in the domain which Sri Aurobindo has termed the Overmind. And from there they presided over the creation of the material universe and the earth. And one of the proceedings was the formation of the earth as a symbolic creation representative of the whole universe, in order to condense and concentrate the problem so that it might be solved more easily. And this earth, though it may be from the astronomical point of view something infinitesimal and as unimportant as can be, from the occult point of view of the universal creation it is a symbol which represents the universe so perfectly that by transforming the earth one can through contagion or analogy transform the universe, because the earth is the symbol of the universe. This was the procedure adopted by the gods. And the place that's the seat of existence of these gods Sri Aurobindo has called the Overmind.

Of course things are not like that. Don't think that I have just told you the story as it really happened. Things are not like that, but it's a way of speaking, a way of making them understandable to the brain. It appears to have occurred like that.

18th May 1955

Questions and Answers, 1955, CWM 2nd Ed., Vol. 7, pp. 157-58

THE STORY OF CREATION

From where do the gods come?

THAT means? . . . "From where" means what? What is their origin? Who has formed them? . . . But everything, everything comes from the one Origin, from the Supreme, the gods also.

There is a very old tradition which narrates this. I am going to tell you the story as one does to children, for in this way you will understand: One day "God" decided to exteriorise himself, objectivise himself, in order to have the joy of knowing himself in detail. So, first of all, he emanated his consciousness (that is to say, he manifested his consciousness) by ordering this consciousness to realise a universe.

This consciousness began by emanating four beings, four individualities which were indeed altogether very high beings, of the highest Reality. They were the being of consciousness, the being of love (of Ananda rather), the being of life and the being of light and knowledge — but consciousness and light are the same thing. There we are then: consciousness, love and Ananda, life and truth — truth, that's the exact word. And naturally, they were supremely powerful beings, you understand.

They were what are called in that tradition the first emanations, that is, the first formations. And each one became very conscious of its qualities, its power, its capacities, its possibilities, and, suddenly forgot each in its own way that it was only an emanation and an incarnation of the Supreme. And so this is what happened: when light or Consciousness separated from the divine Consciousness, that is, when it began to think it was the divine Consciousness and that there was nothing other than itself, it suddenly became obscurity and inconscience.

And when Life thought that all life was in itself and that there was nothing else but its life and that it did not depend at all upon the Supreme, then its life became death. And when Truth thought that it contained all truth, and that there was no other truth than itself, this Truth became falsehood. And when love or Ananda was convinced that it was the supreme Ananda and that there was no other than itself and its felicity, it became suffering. And that is how the world, which was to have been so beautiful, became so ugly. Now, that consciousness (if you like to call it the Divine Mother, the Supreme Consciousness), when she saw this she was very disturbed, you may be sure, she said to herself: "This has really not succeeded." So she turned back to the Divine, to God, the Supreme, and she asked him to come to her aid. She said to him: "This is what has happened. Now what is to be done?" He said: "Begin again, but try to manage in such a way that the beings do not become so independent! . . . They must remain in contact with you, and through you with me."

And it was thus that she created the gods, who were quite docile and not so proud, and who began the creation of the world. But as the others had come before them, at every step the gods met the others. And it was in this way that the world changed into a battlefield, a place of war, strife, suffering, darkness and all the rest, and for each new creation the gods had to fight with the others who had gone ahead: they had preceded them, they had plunged headlong into matter; and they had created all this disorder and the gods had to put straight all this confusion.

That is where the gods came from. They are the second emanations.

Mother, the first four who changed, was it by chance or was it deliberately?

No. What is chance?

    It is said also — that is the continuation of the story or rather its beginning — that the Divine wanted his creation to be a free creation. He wanted all that went forth from him to be absolutely independent and free in order to be able to unite with him in freedom, not through compulsion. He did not want that they should be compelled to be faithful, compelled to be conscious, compelled to be obedient. They had to do it spontaneously, through the knowledge and conviction that that was much better. So this world was created as a world of total freedom, freedom of choice. And it is in this way that at every moment everyone has the freedom of choice — but with all the consequences. If one chooses well, it is good, but if one chooses ill, ah well, what's to happen happens — that is what has happened!

    The story may be understood in a much more occult and spiritual sense. But it is like all the stories of the universe: if you want to narrate them so that people may understand, they become stories for children. But if one knows how to see the truth behind the symbols, one understands everything. Even with what I have told you, which seems like a little story for children, even like that, if you understand what I have told you and the meaning of what I have told you, you can have the secret of things.

There are traditions which say that it is an "accident", in the sense that it could have been otherwise. But it happened like that. It is true, it came about like that. Only, it was quite understandable that every one of these elements having its origin in the Supreme, being quite close to the Emanation at that moment, quite close to the Origin, carried in itself the consciousness of its divinity and superiority, necessarily, since this is not a creation made with something foreign to the Divine: it is simply the Divine who has emanated himself, as though he were looking at himself — he objectivises himself in order to become aware of all that he is; instead of being in an inner static state of concentration in which all is unmanifested, he projects that outside himself "in order to see", as though he wanted to see all that is within him, that is, all the infinity of possibilities. So, all was possible. It happened like that — it could have happened otherwise. Besides, nothing tells you that alongside our universe such as it is, there do not exist others which are so different that there cannot be any relation between one universe and another. It can very well be that our universe is not the only exteriorisation of the Divine. Ours is such as we know it; there may be others which are in much less sorry a state than this one! Besides, it is lamentable only in its appearance. If you go behind the appearance, you become aware that it is not lamentable at all. It is only one way of seeing.

25th November 1953

Questions and Answers, 1953, CWM 2nd Ed., Vol. 5, pp. 371-75

DIVINE LOVE DESCENDED
INTO MATTER

You say, "Love is everywhere. Its movement is there in plants, perhaps in the very stones. . . ."[1] If there is love in a stone, how can one see it?

PERHAPS *the different elements constituting the stone are coordinated by the spark of love. I am sure that when the Divine Love descended into Matter, this Matter was quite unconscious, it had absolutely no form; it may even be said that forms in general are the result of the effort of Love to bring consciousness into Matter. If one of you (I have my doubts, but still) went down into the Inconscient, what is called the pure Inconscient, you would realise what it is. A stone will seem to you a marvellously conscious object in comparison. You speak disdainfully of a stone because you have just a wee bit more consciousness than it has, but the difference between the consciousness of the stone and the total Inconscient is perhaps greater than that between the stone and you. And the coming out of the Inconscient is due exclusively to the sacrifice of the Divine, to this descent of divine Love into the Inconscient. Consequently, when I said "perhaps in the stone", I could*

---

1. *Questions and Answers, 1929, 2 June.*

have removed the "perhaps" — I can assert that even in the stone it is there. There would be nothing, neither stone nor metal nor any organisation of atoms without this presence of Divine Love.

Most people say there is "consciousness" when they begin to think — when one doesn't think one is not conscious. But plants are perfectly conscious and yet they do not think. They have very precise sensations which are the expression of a consciousness, but they do not think. Animals begin to think and their reactions are much more complex. But both plants and animals are conscious. One can be conscious of a sensation without having the least thought.

Did material substance exist before the descent of Divine Love?

I don't think it could be said that there was a material substance. The Inconscient . . . is the Inconscient. I don't know how to explain this to you. If there is a negation of something, it is truly the Inconscient, it is the negation of everything. It has not even the capacity of emptiness. One needs to have descended there to know what it is and explain it. Words cannot describe it. It is the negation of all things because everything begins with consciousness. Without consciousness there is nothing.

Were there any beings before this descent of Love? Were they conscious?

There were no terrestrial beings. The terrestrial world, the earth came into existence after the descent into the Inconscient, not before.

The gradual formation of the different stages of being, from the Supreme to the most material region, is subsequent to the Inconscient. When, precisely, the Consciousness "began" its creation (don't take what I say quite literally as though it were a little history of another country, for it is not that, I am trying to make you understand, that's all), the first manifestation of the creative Consciousness was just an emanation of consciousness — of conscious light — and when this emanation separated itself from its origin, the Inconscient was born, through opposition (how to put it?) yes, really through opposition. Consequently, the birth of the Inconscient is prior to the formation of the world, and it was only when the perception came that the whole universe was going to be created uselessly that there was a call and Divine Love plunged into the Inconscient to change it into consciousness. Therefore, it can be said that the formation of the material worlds as we know them is the result of the descent of the supreme Consciousness into the Inconscient. It cannot be said that there was something prior to that, things as we know them in the material world (I apologise for the ambiguity of my words, but you understand one cannot express these things in our usual words).

The formation of the earth as we know it, this infinitesimal point in the immense universe, was made precisely in order to concentrate the effort of transformation upon one point; it is like a symbolic point created in the universe to make it possible, while working directly upon one point, to radiate it over the entire universe.

If we want to make the problem a little more comprehensible, it is enough to limit ourselves to the creation and the history of the earth, for it is a good symbol of universal history.

From the astronomical point of view the earth is nothing, it is a very small accident. From the spiritual point of view, it is a symbolic willed formation. And as I have already said, *it is only upon earth that this Presence is found, this direct contact with the supreme Origin, this presence of the divine Consciousness hidden in all things.*

The other worlds have been organised more or less hierarchically, if one may say so, but the earth has a special formation due to the direct intervention, without any intermediary, of the supreme Consciousness in the Inconscient.

24th March 1951

Questions and Answers, 1950-51, CWM 2nd Ed., Vol. 4, pp. 240-42

International Publications

Auroville Architecture
by Franz Fassbender

Auroville Form Style and Design
by Franz Fassbender

Landscapes and Gardens of Auroville
by Franz Fassbender

Inauguration of Auroville
by Franz Fassbender

Auroville in a Nutshell
by Tim Wrey

Death doesn't exist
The Mother on Death, Sri Aurobindo on Rebirth
Compiled by Franz Fassbender

Divine Love
Compiled by Franz Fassbender

Five Dream
by Sri Aurobindo

A Vision
Compiled by Franz Fassbender

Passage to More than India
by Dick Batstone

The Mother on Japan
Compiled by Franz Fassbender

Children of Change: A Spiritual Pilgrimage
by Amrit (Howard Shoji Iriyama)

Memories of Auroville - told by early Aurovilians
by Janet Feran

The Journeying Years
by Dianna Bowler

Auroville Reflected
by Bindu Mohanty

Finding the Psychic Being
by Loretta Shartsis

The Teachings of Flowers
The Life and Work of the Mother of the Sri Aurobindo
Ashram
by Loretta Shartsis

The Supramental Transformation
by Loretta Shartsis

The Mother's Yoga - 1956-1973 (English & French)
Vol. 1, 1956-1967 & Vol. 2, 1968-1973
by Loretta Shartsis

Antithesis of Yoga
by Jocelyn Janaka

Bougainvilleas PROTECTION
by Narad (Richard Eggenberger), Nilisha Mehta

Crossroad The New Humanity
by Paulette Hadnagy

Die Praxis Des Integralen Yoga
by M. P. Pandit

The Way of the Sunlit Path
by William Sullivan

Wildlife great and small of India's Coromandel
by Tim Wrey

A New Education With A Soul
by Marguerite Smithwhite

Featured Titles

Divine Love

The texts presented in this book are selected from the Mother and Sri Aurobindo.
"Awakened to the meaning of my heart. That to feel love and oneness is to live. And this the magic of our golden change, is all the truth I know or seek, O sage."

Sri Aurobindo, Savitri, Book XII, Epilog

A Vision by the Mother

On 28th May 1958, the Mother recounted a vision she once had of a wonderful Being of Love and Consciousness, emanated from the Supreme Origin and projected directly into the Inconscient so that the creation would gradually awaken to the Supramental Consciousness. The Mother's account of this vision was brought out a first time in November 1906, in the Revue Cosmique, a monthly review published in Paris.

A Dream – Aims and Ideals of Auroville
the Mother on Auroville

50 years of Auroville from 28.02.1968 - 28.02.2018
Today, information about Auroville is abundant. Many people try to make meaning out of Auroville – about its conception, to what direction should we grow towards, and, what are we doing here?

But what was Mother's original Dream and what was her Vision for Auroville back then?

Matrimandir Talks by the Mother

This book presents most of Mother's Matrimandir talks, including how she conceived the idea for this special concentration and meditation building in Auroville.

Memories of Auroville - Told by early Aurovilians

Memories of Auroville is a book about the very early days of Auroville based on interviews made in 1997 with Aurovilians who lived here between 1968 and 1973. The interviews presented in this book are part of a history program for newcomers that I had created with my friend, Philip Melville in 1997. The plan was to divide Auroville's history into different eras and then interview Aurovilians according to their area of knowledge. Our first section would cover the years from 1968 till 1973 when the Mother was still in her physical body.

The Way of the Sunlit Path

May The Way of the Sunlit Path be a convenient guide for activating this ancient truth as a support for a Conscious Evolution.
May it illumine the transformation offered to us in the Integral Yoga.

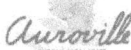

A Dream Takes Shape (in English, French, Hindi)

A comprehensive brochure on the international township of Auroville in, ranging from its Charter and "Why Auroville?" to the plan of the township, the central Matrimandir, the national pavilions and residences, to working groups, the economy, making visits, how to join, its relationship to the Sri Aurobindo Ashram, and its key role in the future of the world. This brochure endeavours to highlight how The Mother envisioned Auroville from its inception, some of the major achievements realised over the years, and some of the currently faced in implementing the guidelines which she gave.

Mother on Japan

I had everything to learn in Japan. For four years, from an artistic point of view, I lived from wonder to wonder. And everything in this city, in this country, from beginning to end, gives you the impression of impermanence, of the unexpected, the exceptional... ...everything in this city, in this country, from beginning to end, gives you the impression of impermanence, of the unexpected, the exceptional. You always come to things you did not expect, you want to find them again and they are lost – they have made something else which is equally charming.

Auroville Reflected

On 28 February 1968, on an impoverished plateau on the Coromandel Coast of South India, about 4,000 people from around the world gathered for a most unusual inauguration. Handfuls of soil from the countries of the world were mixed together as a symbol of human unity. Why did Indira Gandhi, the erstwhile Prime Minister of India, support this development for "a city the earth needs?" Why did UNESCO endorse this project? Why does the Dalai Lama continue to be involved in the project? What led anthropologist Margaret Mead to insist that records must be kept of its progress? Why did both historian William Irwin Thompson and United Nations representative Robert Muller note that this social experiment may be a breakthrough for humanity even as critics commented, "it is an impossible dream"?

A House For the Third Millennium
Essays on Matrimandir

Nightwatch at the Matrimandir...
A cosmic spectacle; the black expanse above, the big black crater of Matrimandir's excavation carved deep into the soil. The four pillars - two of which are completed and the other two nearing completion - are four huge ships coming together from the four corners of the earth to meet at this pro propitious spot...

Passage to More than India

This book is a voyage of discovery. In 1959 the author, Dick Batstone, a classically educated bookseller in England, with a Christian background, comes across a life of the great Indian polymath Sri Aurobindo, though a series of apparently fortuitous circumstances. A meeting in Durham, England, leads him to a determination to get to the Sri Aurobindo Ashram in Pondicherry, a former French territory south of Madras.

www.ingramcontent.com/pod-product-compliance
Lightning Source LLC
Chambersburg PA
CBHW080350241125
35547CB00077B/1952